My Song
Is
Beautiful

Poems and Pictures
in Many Voices

Selected by
**Mary Ann
Hoberman**

LITTLE, BROWN AND COMPANY
Books for Young Readers
New York   Boston

In memory of Jesse Murry

Acknowledgments • Thanks are given as follows for permission to reprint copyrighted material: **Mary Austin:** "A Song of Greatness" from *The Children Sing in the Far West*, by Mary Austin. Copyright © 1928 by Mary Austin; copyright © renewed 1956 by Kenneth M. Chapman and Mary C. Wheelwright. Reprinted by permission of Houghton Mifflin Harcourt Publishing Company. All rights reserved. **Toni de Gerez:** "My Song" from *My Song Is a Piece of Jade: Poems of Ancient Mexico in English and Spanish*, adapted by Toni de Gerez. English translation copyright © 1984 by Organización Editorial Novaro, S. A. Reprinted by permission of Little, Brown and Company. **Nikki Giovanni:** "drum" from *Spin a Soft Black Song*, revised edition, by Nikki Giovanni. Copyright © 1971, 1985 by Nikki Giovanni. Reprinted by permission of Hill and Wang, a division of Farrar, Straus and Giroux, LLC. **Nicole Hernandez:** "No Shadow in the Water." Copyright © 1992 by Nicole Hernandez. Reprinted by permission of the author. **Felice Holman:** "Who Am I?" from *At the Top of My Voice and Other Poems*, by Felice Holman. Copyright © 1970 by Felice Holman. Reprinted by permission of the author. **James Houston:** "Ayii, Ayii, Ayii" from *Songs of the Dream People: Chants and Images from the Indians and Eskimos of North America*, edited and illustrated by James Houston. Copyright © 1972 by James Houston. Reprinted by permission of Saumik, LLC. **Langston Hughes:** "Birth" from *The Collected Poems of Langston Hughes*, by Langston Hughes, edited by Arnold Rampersad with David Roessel, Associate Editor, copyright © 1994 by the Estate of Langston Hughes. Used by permission of Alfred A. Knopf, a division of Random House, Inc. (U.S., Canada, P.I.) and Harold Ober Associates (U.K.). **Ruth Krauss:** "Beginning on Paper," reprinted by permission of the author. **Karla Kuskin:** "Me" from *Alexander Soames: His Poems*. Copyright © 1962, 1980 by Karla Kuskin. Reprinted by permission of S©ott Treimel NY. **A. A. Milne:** "The End" from *Now We Are Six*, by A. A. Milne, illustrated by E. H. Shepard, copyright © 1927 by E. P. Dutton, renewed © 1955 by A. A. Milne. Reprinted by permission of www.penguin.com (U.S., Canada, P.I.). All rights reserved. "The End" from *Now We Are Six*, by A. A. Milne. Copyright © The Trustees of Pooh Properties. Published by Egmont UK, Ltd. London and used with permission (world, excluding U.S. and Canada). **Jack Prelutsky:** "Me I Am" from *The Random House Book of Poetry for Children*, selected and introduced by Jack Prelutsky. Copyright © 1983 by Jack Prelutsky. Reprinted by permission of the author. **Michael Rosen:** "I Know Someone" from *Quick, Let's Get Out of Here*, by Michael Rosen, illustrated by Quentin Blake (Andrew Deutsch 1983, Puffin 2006). Copyright © 1983 by Michael Rosen. Reprinted by permission of United Agents (www.unitedagents.co.uk) on behalf of Michael Rosen (U.S., P.I.) and Penguin Books, Ltd. (world, excluding U.S. and P.I.). **Kim Soo-Jang:** "In a Hermit's Cottage," from *Sunset in a Spider Web: Sijo Poetry of Ancient Korea*, by Kim Soo-Jang, adapted by Virginia Olsen Baron. Copyright © 1974 by Virginia Olsen Baron. Reprinted by permission of Virginia Olsen Baron (British Commonwealth) and Henry Holt and Company, LLC (world, excluding British Commonwealth).

Library of Congress Cataloging-in-Publication Data

My song is beautiful : poems and pictures in many voices / selected by Mary Ann Hoberman — 1st ed.
   p. cm.
  ISBN 978-0-316-06835-2
  1. Children's poetry.   [1. Poetry — Collections.]   I. Hoberman, Mary Ann.
  PN6109.97.M9   1994
  808.81'0083 — dc20

10 9 8 7 6 5 4 3 2 1

WOR

Printed in the United States of America

CONTENTS

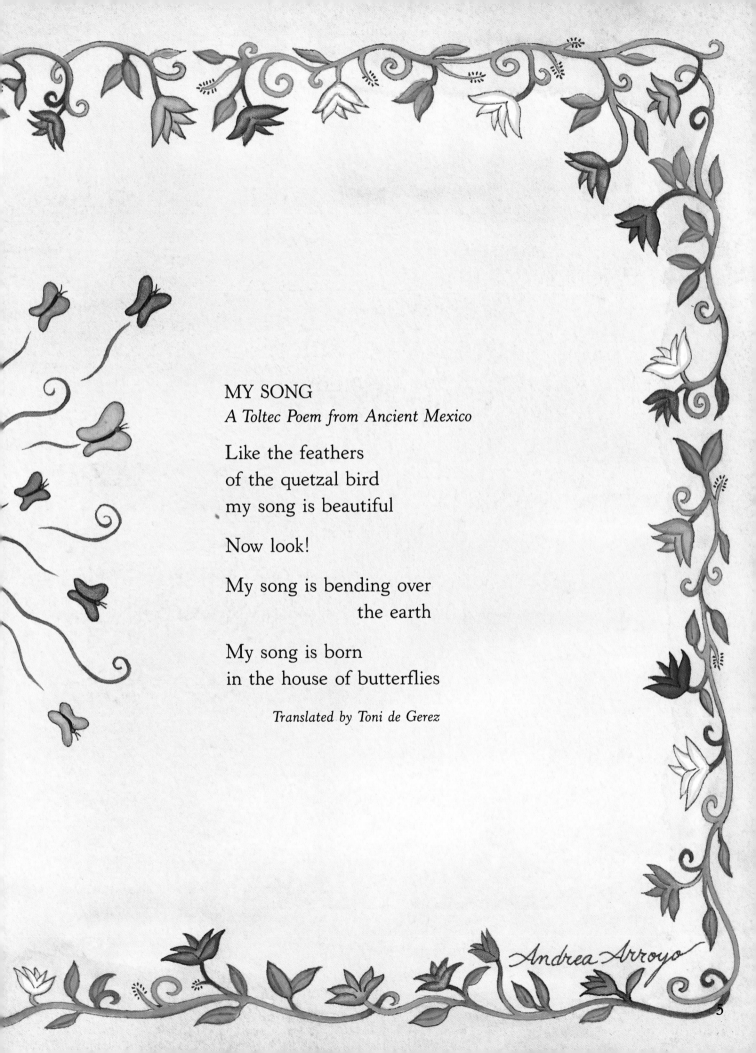

MY SONG
A Toltec Poem from Ancient Mexico

Like the feathers
of the quetzal bird
my song is beautiful

Now look!

My song is bending over
                    the earth

My song is born
in the house of butterflies

Translated by Toni de Gerez

BIRTH

Oh, fields of wonder
Out of which
Stars are born,
And moon and sun
And me as well,
Like stroke
Of lightning
In the night
Some mark
To make
Some word
To tell.

— *Langston Hughes*

BEGINNING ON PAPER

on paper
I write it
on rain

I write it
on stones
on my boots

on trees
I write it
on the air

on the city
how pretty
I write my name

— *Ruth Krauss*

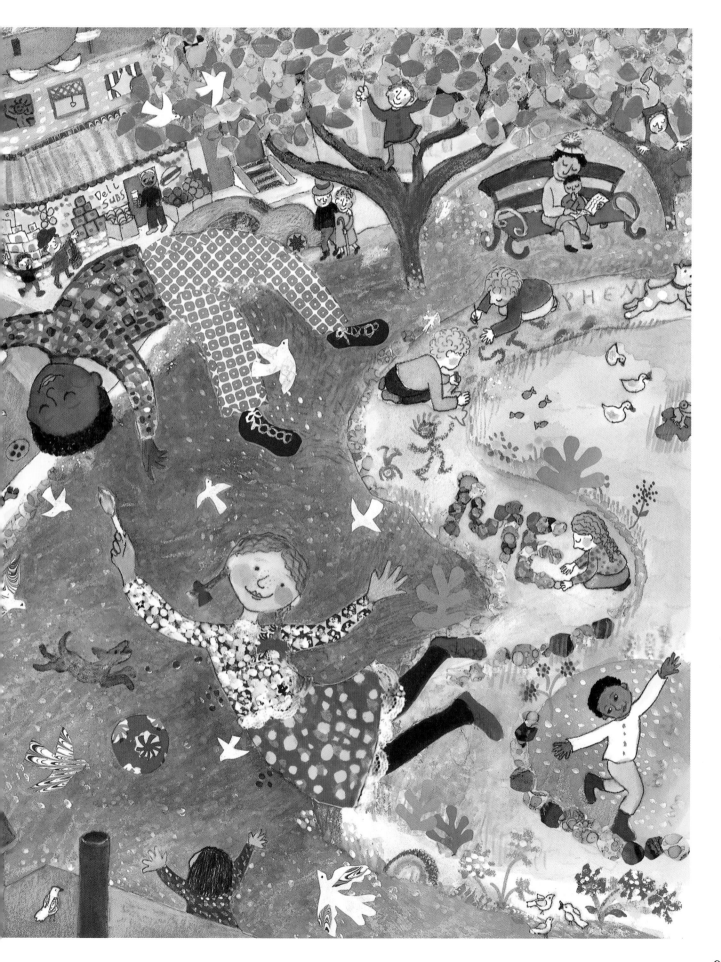

ME

"My nose is blue,
My teeth are green,
My face is like a soup tureen.
I look just like a lima bean.
I'm very, very lovely.
My feet are far too short
And long.
My hands are left and right
And wrong.
My voice is like the hippo's song.
I'm very, very,
Very, very,
Very, very
Lovely?"

— *Karla Kuskin*

THE DRUM

daddy says the world is
a drum tight and hard
and i told him
i'm gonna beat
out my own rhythm

— *Nikki Giovanni*

A SONG OF GREATNESS
A Chippewa Indian Song

When I hear the old men
Telling of heroes,
Telling of great deeds
Of ancient days,
When I hear them telling,
Then I think within me
I too am one of these.

When I hear the people
Praising great ones,
Then I know that I too
Shall be esteemed,
I too when my time comes
Shall do mightily.

Translated by Mary Austin

ME I AM!

I am the only ME I AM
who qualifies as me;
no ME I AM has been before,
and none will ever be.

No other ME I AM can feel
the feelings I've within;
no other ME I AM can fit
precisely in my skin.

There is no other ME I AM
who thinks the thoughts I do;
the world contains one ME I AM,
there is no room for two.

I am the only ME I AM
this earth shall ever see;
that ME I AM I always am
is no one else but ME!

— *Jack Prelutsky*

I KNOW SOMEONE

I know someone who can
take a mouthful of custard and blow it
down their nose.

I know someone who can
make their ears wiggle.
I know someone who can
shake their cheeks so it sounds
like ducks quacking.

I know someone who can
throw peanuts in the air and catch them
in their mouth.

I know someone who can
balance a pile of 12 pennies on his elbow
and snatch his elbow from under them
and catch them.

I know someone who can
bend her thumb back to touch her wrist.

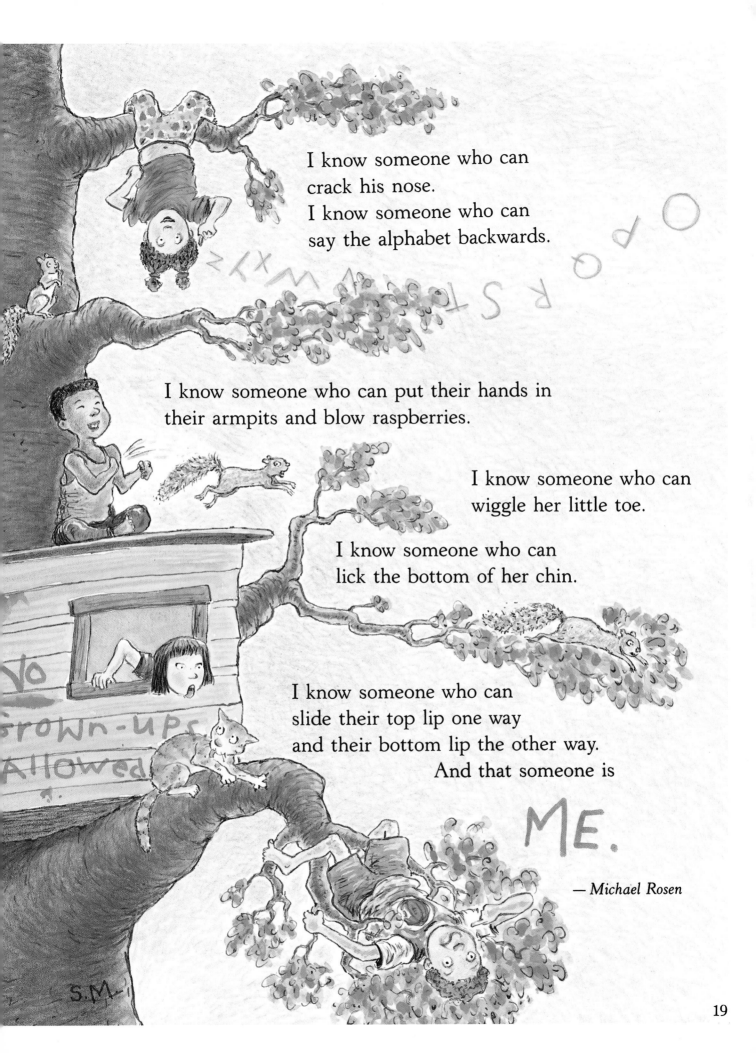

I know someone who can
crack his nose.
I know someone who can
say the alphabet backwards.

I know someone who can put their hands in
their armpits and blow raspberries.

I know someone who can
wiggle her little toe.

I know someone who can
lick the bottom of her chin.

I know someone who can
slide their top lip one way
and their bottom lip the other way.
And that someone is

ME.

— *Michael Rosen*

19

AYII, AYII, AYII
An Inuit Chant from the Central Arctic

Ayii, ayii, ayii,
My arms, they wave high in the air,
My hands, they flutter behind my back,
They wave above my head
Like the wings of a bird.
Let me move my feet.
Let me dance.
Let me shrug my shoulders.
Let me shake my body.
Let me crouch down.
My arms, let me fold them.
Let me hold my hands under my chin.

Translated by James Houston

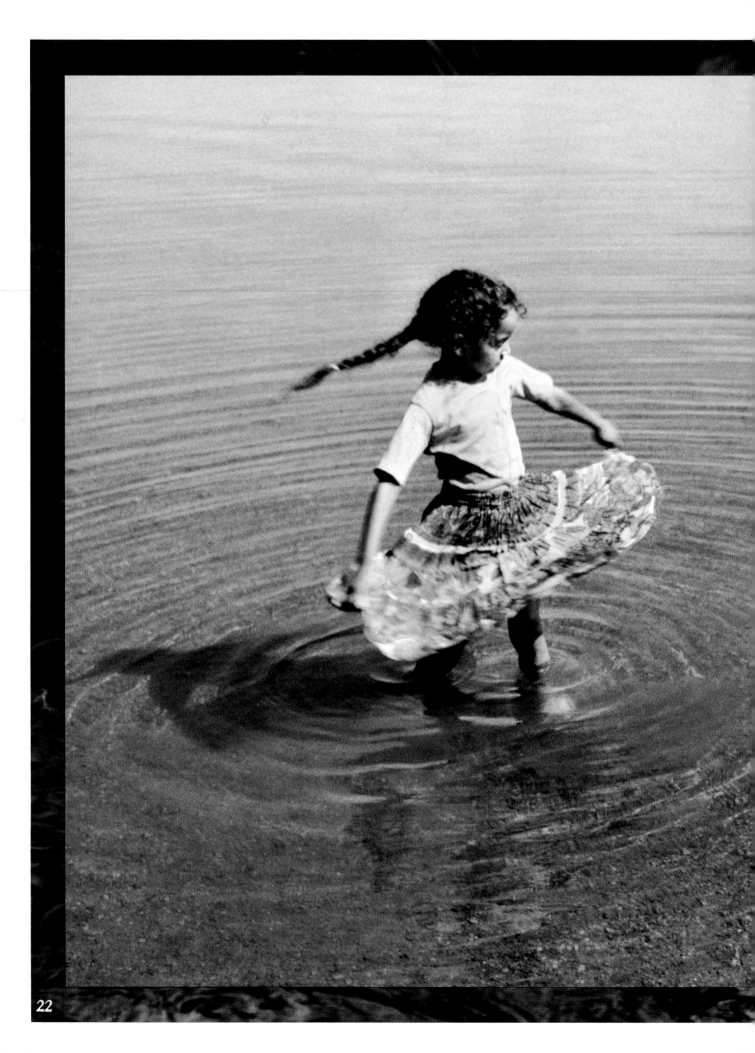

NO SHADOW IN THE WATER

I see myself
in the water
and my face
is shining
down
deep.

— *Nicole Hernandez*

Carol Palmer

YOU AND I

Only one I in the whole wide world
And millions and millions of you,
But every you is an I to itself
And I am a you to you, too!

But if I am a you and you are an I
And the opposite also is true,
It makes us both the same somehow
Yet splits us each in two.

It's more and more mysterious,
The more I think it through:
Every you everywhere in the world is an I;
Every I in the world is a you!

        — Mary Ann Hoberman

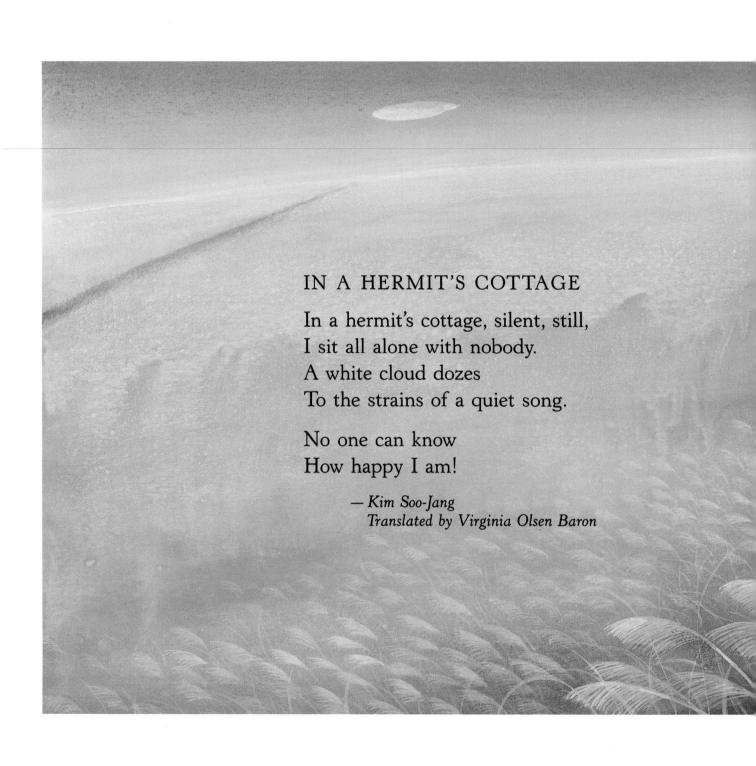

IN A HERMIT'S COTTAGE

In a hermit's cottage, silent, still,
I sit all alone with nobody.
A white cloud dozes
To the strains of a quiet song.

No one can know
How happy I am!

— *Kim Soo-Jang*
Translated by Virginia Olsen Baron

WHO AM I?

The trees ask me,
And the sky,
And the sea asks me
    Who am I?

The grass asks me,
And the sand,
And the rocks ask me
    Who am I?

The wind tells me
At nightfall,
And the rain tells me
    Someone small.

    Someone small
    Someone small
    But a piece
           of
           it
           all.

        — *Felice Holman*

THE END

When I was One,
I had just begun.

When I was Two,
I was nearly new.

When I was Three,
I was hardly Me.

When I was Four,
I was not much more.

When I was Five,
I was just alive.

But now I am Six, I'm as clever as clever.
So I think I'll be six now for ever and ever.

— *A. A. Milne*

NOTES ON THE POETS AND ARTISTS

Andrea Arroyo is a Mexican artist whose work has regularly appeared in *The New Yorker* and the *New York Times*. Her illustration is in watercolor and ink on paper.

Mary Austin (1868–1934) was a writer committed to the preservation of Native American folklore. She translated the poem here from Chippewa.

Ashley Bryan has won the Coretta Scott King Award multiple times for his books, including *Beat the Story-Drum, Pum-Pum*, a retelling of African folktales; and *Let It Shine: Three Favorite Spirituals*. His painting is in tempera and gouache.

Dale DeArmond (1914–2006) published many books based on the mythology of the native people of Alaska, her home. Her piece is a wood engraving cut in an end-grain maple block and printed in a manually operated etching press.

Toni de Gerez has lived all over Latin America, lecturing and writing on native mythology and verse. She translated the poem included here, which was sung in magical ceremonies by the Toltec people of ancient Mexico, from the original Náhuatl language.

Catherine De Vuono guided elementary students from Brooklyn P.S. 16 in creating the self-portrait quilt featured here, which is composed of painted fabric stitch-sewn together. The young artists who contributed to this piece are: F. Davis, J. Negron, K. Pagan, A. Guzzman, C. Seetram, A. Fowler, N. Salim, E. Shafidiya, T. Jie, B. Rahaman, M. Resto, and M. Bayne.

David Diaz's artwork is a silk-screen print to which watercolors have been applied. He is the illustrator of *Smoky Night*, for which he won the Caldecott Medal.

Bernie Fuchs's painting was done in oil on canvas. The illustrator of several picture books, he has also painted portraits of U.S. presidents, athletes, and celebrities and has received over one hundred awards for his work.

Nikki Giovanni is one of the best-known figures of the New Black Poetry and has written many books, including *Rosa*, which won the Caldecott Medal and the Coretta Scott King Medal.

Nicole Hernandez was a seventh-grader at Junior High School 126 in Brooklyn when her poem was chosen from the Inner Cities Arts Project, run by teacher Jeffrey Pflaum.

Mary Ann Hoberman wrote her poem "You and I" especially for this anthology, of which she is also the editor.

Felice Holman has received many honors throughout her long and prolific career, including an American Library Association notable book citation for *Slake's Limbo*.

James Houston (1921–2005) lived in the Arctic among the Inuit (Canadian Eskimos) for fourteen years and wrote about their songs and stories in numerous children's books, two of which won the Book of the Year for Children Award by the Canadian Library Association.

Langston Hughes (1902–1967) was a celebrated African-American poet, novelist, playwright and short story writer and was a significant voice in the Harlem Renaissance.

Yoriko Ito was born and raised in Mie, Japan. She has illustrated several picture books, including *Silver Charm: A Folktale from Japan*. Her piece was done in acrylic and mixed media.

Elisa Kleven is self-taught and works in a mixed-media collage technique, reminiscent of the way she used and compiled materials in her childhood creations. Books she has illustrated include *de Colores and Other Latin American Folk Songs for Children*.

Ruth Krauss (1903–1933) is the author of the classic children's books *The Carrot Seed* and *A Hole Is to Dig*.

Karla Kuskin is an award-winning poet whose collections include *Dogs and Dragons, Trees and Dreams*.

David McPhail's numerous picture books include *Edward and the Pirates* and *Santa's Book of Names*. His illustration was done in pen-and-ink and watercolor.

Holly Meade's award-winning books include the Caldecott Honor Book *Hush! A Thai Lullaby*. She used a combination of silk-screen printing and gouache painting to create her piece.

Susan Meddaugh's art is a combination of pen-and-ink, watercolor, and colored pencils. She is the creator of *Martha Speaks*, a *New York Times* Best Illustrated Book.

A. A. Milne (1882–1956) is best known for his beloved Winnie-the-Pooh books as well as his collections of verse for children.

Keiko Narahashi's artwork is in watercolor. She is the illustrator of a number of picture books, including *The Magic Purse*, a Japanese folktale by Yoshiko Uchida.

Carol Palmer hand-tints her black-and-white photographs. She often exhibits her pictures of children and their families in New England.

Jack Prelutsky has over fifty volumes of poetry collections to his name. In 2006 the Poetry Foundation named him the first U.S. children's poet laureate.

Michael Rosen is both a children's novelist and poet and the author of 140 books. In 2007 he was appointed the U.K.'s fifth children's laureate.

Irana Shepherd's illustration was created with a combination of watercolor, gouache, and pastel. Her artwork appears in children's books, games, and cards.

Kim Soo-Jang's poem is a Sijo poem, one of the earliest and most popular forms of Korean verse. It was translated by Virginia Olsen Baron, the editor of several anthologies of Asian poetry.